Snakes and Lizards

Edward and Clive Turner

Priory Press Limited

Young Naturalist Books

Squirrels
Foxes
Bats
Rabbits and Hares
Hedgehogs
Badgers
Rats and Mice
Deer
Frogs and Toads
Spiders
Stoats and Weasels
Otters
Bees and Wasps
Birds of Prey
Snakes and Lizards

SBN 85078 174 4
Copyright © 1974 Edward & Clive Turner and Priory Press Ltd
First published in 1974 by
Priory Press Ltd
101 Grays Inn Rd, London WC1

Filmset by Keyspools Ltd, Golborne, Lancs
Printed in Great Britain by
The Pitman Press, Bath.

Contents

An Aesculapian snake from Southern Europe, ready to strike.

Snakes and Lizards

Frontispiece: *A giant lizard: a* komodo dragon *from Indonesia.*

1: "Upon Thy Belly Shalt Thou Go"

To primitive people the snake must have appeared a mysterious creature. The animal seemed wise because its eyes always stayed open with a piercing and unblinking stare. Another curious thing about the snake was the way that it shed its old skin in one piece. As the bright skin underneath shines like new, all snakes were thought to be immortal.

Snakes also move in a strange way, without any legs. Even more alarming, they could inflict sudden death on humans. It is no wonder that the snake was respected and even worshipped by early civilizations all over the world.

The ancient Egyptians thought that their own gods had descended from snakes and were therefore very powerful beings. Statues of the pharaohs usually had a cobra called *Wadget* fixed to their foreheads. Many other early

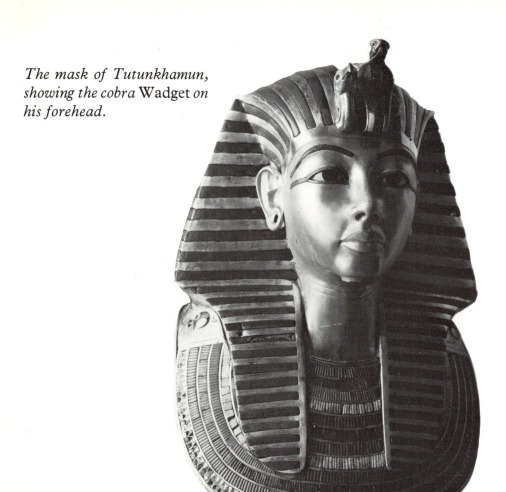

The mask of Tutunkhamun, showing the cobra Wadget *on his forehead.*

cultures, including the Aztecs and the North American Indians, worshipped the snake as a bringer of rain and a source of fertility. This belief is still held by some African Bushmen and Australian Aborigines. The name of one Aborigine snake god is *Mindi*. This fearful character is said to be ten miles long and have the unpleasant habit of carrying smallpox.

This lizard, called **Boyd's forest dragon,** *looks as though it still lives in prehistoric times.*

The story of the Garden of Eden gave the snake a reputation it does not deserve. In the passage from the Bible the snake appeared as the infamous messenger of the Devil and tempted Eve with the forbidden apple. God is said to have punished this evil deed by taking away the snake's legs. Before this awful punishment the snake was supposed to have had legs and possibly wings as well. It sounds a sinister creature rather like the dragons in fairy tales.

Most people have heard of the remarkable dinosaurs

A girdle-tailed lizard *from Madascar, in the Indian Ocean.*

which roamed the surface of the earth long before man appeared. But few of us may realize that the snakes and lizards of today are surviving relatives of these extinct creatures.

It may seem a little odd to write about snakes and lizards in the same book. Surely the legless snake has nothing in common with the lizard, which walks about like any other four-legged animal? It is only when we look very carefully at them both that we see that they share some unusual features and ways of life.

Another strange-looking monster called Goniocephalus, *from Malaya.*

With their more distant relatives the tortoises, crocodiles and the long dead dinosaurs, the snakes and lizards are called *reptiles*. In this book we shall try to unravel some of the mysteries that have always surrounded these fascinating animals.

The *carboniferous* period started about 270 million years ago and lasted for 60 million years. During this long period of time, lowland swamps covered much of the land. These wet areas were important because coal was formed from the remains of dead plants. They also provided a suitable home for the simplest four-legged animals, the *amphibians*.

Some of the ancient amphibians were like frogs, but others were as big as crocodiles. These carboniferous amphibians probably lived near water most of the time.

By the end of the carboniferous period there were animals similar to reptiles. These were strange animals with some amphibian and some reptile features. For instance, the fossil remains of the extinct animal *seymouria* show that its skull shape was like a reptile but its teeth were those of an amphibian. This tells us that reptiles could have gradually developed from an ancient type of amphibian.

Some readers may be wondering how one animal can change into another in this way. The answer is not simple. First, it is important to realize that animals are changing all the time; but these changes are so slight and

13

A drawing of what people think the world looked like 150 million years ago, in the age of the dinosaurs.

slow that they are hardly noticeable.

It is easier to see these changes in our domestic animals, because the process is more rapid. For example, farmers are always trying to breed heavier and more meaty cattle.

14

As a result of carefully choosing their best bulls and breeding from them, prize animals today are more than twice the weight of Victorian prize bulls.

About two million years ago, the early fossil skulls of man show that his brain was only about half the size of ours. In these ancient times the man with the biggest brain would probably be able to work out the best ways of hunting. He would be more successful and would perhaps be able to have more wives and breed more rapidly than the less clever men. Because of this it would not be surprising if the brain gradually grew bigger.

Any part of the body of an animal could change in the same way if the change helped the animal. Over millions of years a number of changes of this sort might take place. So one kind of animal could gradually change into something rather different.

Seventy million years after their first appearance the simple early reptiles had evolved into a variety of fantastic creatures. These included the dinosaurs, the flying pterosaurs and the incredible sea-going plesiosaurs.

Throughout the *mesozoic* period, which lasted 120 million years, the reptiles were the dominant animals. However, quite early on in this period, one important group of reptiles had already evolved. These were curious creatures that could fly short distances using feathers which were really a special kind of reptilian scale. These little animals are thought to have been the

Some extinct reptiles. No. 4 is a sea crocodile; 5 and 8, dinosaurs; 6, a flesh-eating dinosaur; 7, a pterosaur; 9, a duck-billed dinosaur; 11, a plesiosaur; 12, an ichthyosaur; 13, the skull of a prehistoric tortoise; and 17, a mosasaur, a sea lizard ancestor of today's monitor lizard. They all lived between 40 and 160 million years ago. Human beings have only existed for about 1 million years.

The scaly head of the common iguana.

ancestors of the birds. The mammals also evolved from the reptiles, but we do not know exactly when this happened.

The first and most exciting reptiles became extinct by the end of the mesozoic time. The birds probably replaced the flying reptiles, while the mammals slowly filled the gaps left by the extinct sea and land reptiles. Some people think that many reptiles became extinct due to a new, cool, world climate. Later in this book we shall see why such a climate would have been disastrous to the large reptiles, and helped the mammals and birds.

2: Waterproof Coats and Cold Blood

Because snakes and lizards have rather delicate skeletons they rarely become fossilized intact, if at all. But we know that lizards existed alongside the dinosaurs at least 160 million years ago.

The most exciting of these ancient lizards were the extinct *mosasaurs*. These giant sea animals reached an impressive length of sixteen metres. With their huge jaws and teeth it is unlikely that their underwater ferocity has ever been matched.

Early snakes appeared as a development of an unknown mesozoic lizard. It seems that they were not poisonous and may have resembled the pythons of today. It is interesting that the pythons and a few other snakes have very small hind-limb bones. They are not used for walking, but it is good evidence that these snakes have evolved from animals that had legs.

Opposite: *The head of a grass snake, the most common English snake.*

Unlike modern lizards, snakes have no ear drums with which they can pick up sound vibrations in the air. They are also different in having a unique kind of eye which cannot shut. Protection for the eye is provided by a special cap of transparent skin called a *spectacle*.

Some scientists explain these differences by suggesting that the snake first evolved as an underground type of lizard. These animals gradually lost their legs, which would get in the way as they wriggled through their narrow burrows. Another problem of living in a burrow is that grit from the soil would get into the animals' eyes. To avoid this they would probably keep their eyes shut tight. Perhaps the eyelids finally grew together. It is quite a common thing for the eyes of burrowing animals to be small or even lost altogether.

For some reason the snakes found it better to come out of their burrows and live on land again. The skin over the eye formed by the sealed eyelids became clear so that the snake could see again.

Underground the snake also found it more useful to detect ground vibrations rather than sounds. In this way an approaching enemy could very easily be heard. So today the snake has an age-old hearing problem. It can pick up ground vibrations, but it is deaf to ordinary sounds which travel through the air.

Water is a vital part of all living things. This means that any animal or plant that loses too much water will

These pictures show that snakes and lizards can be very alike. Right: *The tiny legs of the* snake lizard *can only be seen when it is turned on its back.* Below: *It looks like a snake, but in fact it is a legless lizard.*

soon die. The first simple organisms that appeared on earth lived underwater, where there was no problem of drying out. But later, when animals started to inhabit the land, they must have found ways of keeping their bodies moist. About 300 million years ago the reptiles developed as the first animals with backbones that could spend their whole lives out of water.

22   *The common chameleon.*

A lizard warms itself in the morning by lying on a sunny stone (see page 25).

On dry land one of the reptiles' most valuable possessions is their skin. This is thick and dry and stops too much water loss in both snakes and lizards. Reptiles can travel long distances on land even in very dry places. On a similar walking trek, an amphibious animal such as a frog would soon really be "dying for a drink." This is partly because the unfortunate amphibians usually have a very thin skin that rapidly leaks water.

Land animals have bodies which are active when they

23

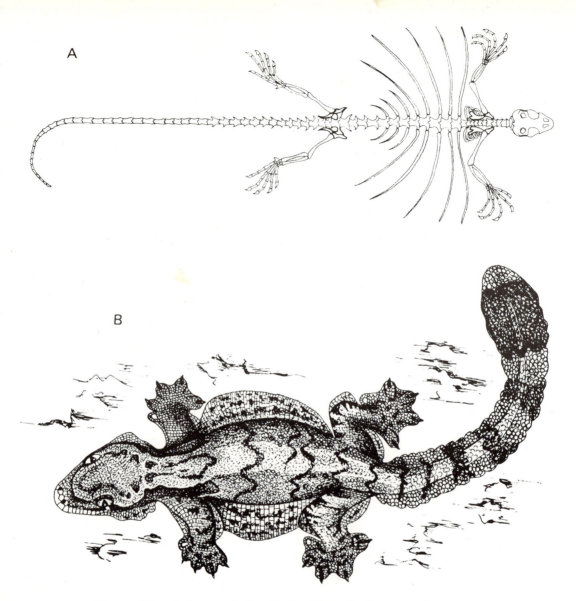

A

B

Top: *The skeleton of the flying lizard,* draco volens; *below:* a *fringed gecko from South-East Asia.*

are warm, but sluggish when too hot or too cold. With the help of their fur or feathers and by other means, mammals and birds can keep their bodies at a steady temperature. This is very helpful in countries where the temperature is often too high or too low.

Snakes, lizards and other reptiles are less complicated animals, and their body temperatures really depend on the weather. If it is a hot day the animal will be hot, and on cold days it will be cold. So it is no wonder that most reptiles live in warm countries. In northern Europe it is usually fairly warm in the daytime, so the animals can stay warm and active for this period.

You may think from this that an animal such as a reptile would die in a very hot or cold climate. It might be chilled or overheated by the weather. But it is surprising to learn that some snakes and lizards live in the hottest deserts, while others manage to live inside the Arctic Circle. Clearly some reptiles have found ways round the dangers of extreme climates.

Before nightfall many lizards and snakes return to their burrows or hiding places. They do this because the cool of the night lowers their body temperature and makes them inactive and helpless. The burrow protects them from their enemies and may also help to keep them snug and warm. In the morning they remain sluggish until the sun warms them up to the temperature when they become active. Like the early bird catching the worm, the first lizard to warm up may get a bonus breakfast. Many lizards get off to a good start by basking on a flat rock which directly faces the morning sun.

Lizards which live in hot climates behave rather like the human inhabitants. They spend a lot of time cooling

25

off in the shade. However, the extreme temperatures of the hot desert day often proves too much for even the craftiest lizards. Luckily, in the desert some warmth from the day lasts a short while after sunset. It is during this time that many nocturnal lizards and snakes are active. Their existence seems dangerous as they have only a short time to find food before the cool night air slows them down.

In colder countries reptiles have a different problem. Even at midday lizards may have to bask in the moderate heat of the sun before becoming warm enough to attempt a feeding expedition. In winter the problems are worse. Snakes and lizards cannot tolerate frost, and there is very little food about. The answer is to *hibernate* through the winter. During this period the animal goes into a very deep sleep in a sheltered nook. It does not usually go out to eat and relies upon the store of fat in its body to keep it alive.

3: Family Life

During the early growth of all backboned animals there is a time when watery surroundings are vital. For instance, the frog tadpole needs to spend all its time in the water until it changes into a frog. At the same stage in the development of reptiles, birds and the mammals, the young are called *embryos*. These are like the tadpole in that they also need a watery home.

Reptiles and birds both lay eggs that are especially suited for hatching out on land. The delicate embryo develops inside the shell in what is really its own private pond. Most tadpoles swim about in an open pond and eat tiny plants, but the embryos of the birds and reptiles absorb their food from the store in the egg yolk. The developing animal remains in the shell until it is ready to hatch. In mammals, which of course include ourselves, the embryo is fed and kept moist inside the body of the mother until it is ready to be born.

Male sea iguanas from the Gala-
pagos Islands fight to win their
mates.

Because they have a tadpole stage, frogs and other amphibians have to live near ponds and streams in order to breed. Reptiles, birds and mammals can live and breed even in dry places. So they are true land animals, while the amphibians are not.

The kind of egg that birds and reptiles lay is protected by a shell which is usually formed around the egg just before it is laid. But the egg cannot develop into a young animal unless it has been fertilized by a male sperm. Fertilization cannot take place, however, once the egg is surrounded by the protective shell. So it is necessary for the male to fertilize the unprotected egg while it is still within the female.

Opposite: *Two pairs of grass snakes mating.*

Family Life

In order to do this, the male has a thing called a *hemipene* which it uses to place the sperm inside the egg opening (the *cloaca*) of the female. In some lizards and snakes, a courtship display may bring the male and female together so that this mating can take place.

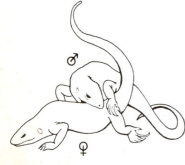

Left and below: *Lizards mating.*

Male snakes and lizards fight for their mates. A shows monitor lizards and B rattlesnakes. Picture E shows the courtship of a pair of king cobras.

y

31

Above: *An Indian grass snake keeps watch over her eggs.* Below:
*Some snakes do not lay eggs but give birth to live young snakes. This
is a water snake with her family of new-born young.*

Snakes and lizards do not have a very sociable life as a family. Usually the eggs are laid and left to hatch out on their own. From the start the little ones have to fend for themselves.

The fierce king cobra shows unexpected concern by building a rough nest for its eggs. Some species of lizard may look after their eggs for a while, and the barking gecko sometimes even tries to look after its young after they have hatched.

One of the oldest serpent stories is about the mother snake who protects her young by swallowing them. When the danger has passed the young snakes crawl out of her mouth again. This behaviour was first reported by a famous naturalist called Gilbert White in the eighteenth century. Even today no one is quite certain how much truth there is in this tale.

Unlike birds, most reptiles are unable to warm their eggs. This is because the temperature of most reptiles is not much higher than their surroundings.

Some female snakes and lizards keep their eggs inside their bodies until they hatch out, and the young are thus born alive. Of those species which have live young, many are found to live in colder regions. It is thought that the mother lies in the sun whenever possible and thus warms the eggs that are inside her. This behaviour may help the eggs to develop more rapidly.

Unlike other sea-going reptiles such as turtles, the sea

13 deadly taipan snakes *just after hatching in New Guinea, in the East Indies.*

snakes bear live young. This is very useful because the adults can live away from land all the time. The turtles have to lay their eggs on land and the young, defenceless turtles suffer very heavy losses from birds when they hatch and make their first dash for the sea.

4: Speed and Size

To escape trouble lizards often rely on a quick sprint. At high speed the fastest lizards use their tails as a balance and run on their hind legs. The champion reptilian sprinter is the South American *basilisk lizard*, which scorches along at 18 miles an hour.

Some of the swiftest snakes are harmless North American racers. Of these, the *coachwhip snake* has been timed at just under 4 m.p.h. A famous reptile expert said of *striped racers*, "I have met them on the deserts and moving so fast we could barely overtake them by running." Perhaps a new turn of speed would have been found if he had been pitted against a more dangerous snake such as the *green mamba*, which is capable of reaching an alarming 6 m.p.h. or more.

It is hard to realize that snakes can possibly make such good times without the use of legs. How do the snakes' wriggling movements drive them forwards?

The most common way of moving is by using side-to-side waves which pass along the body. On a highly polished surface these waves pass along the snake without any effect, but in their natural homes the ground is rough and uneven and the body-waves lock by friction against stones and other objects. The snake moves forward by apparently passing through the locked wave.

Desert sand is not a good surface for the normal method of snake movement. Here a *sidewinding* motion is often used, especially by desert vipers. The snake throws forward one loop at a time to a position beside its head. The animal leaves a J-shaped track.

Some desert lizards have also found interesting ways of moving on sand. For instance, the *fringe-toed lizard* has special feet which can paddle it along at speed through the soft sand.

At sea the only swimming lizard is the *marine iguana*

A basilisk lizard races along on its hind legs.

36

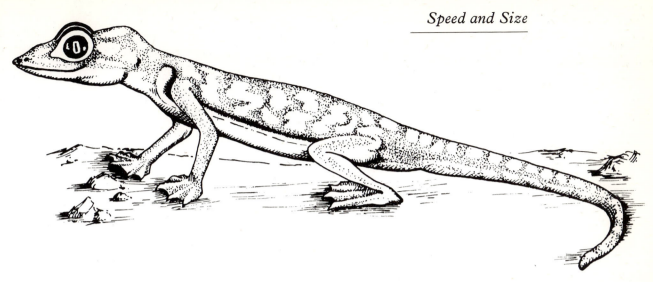

Lizards with special feet for living in the desert. Above: *The feet of the gecko work like snowshoes on snow, and stop the animal sinking into the sand.* Below: *A* fringe-toed skink. *This lizard can dive into the sand and "swim" through it by furiously waggling its body.*

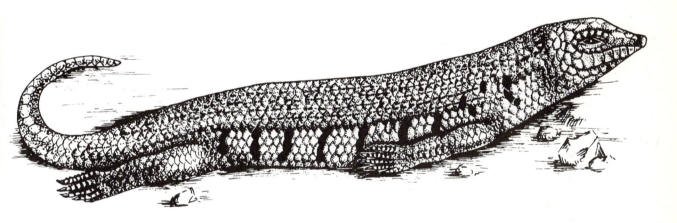

from the Galapagos Islands. Using a long flattened tail and partly webbed feet, this animal is a fine inshore swimmer. *Sea snakes* are more daring voyagers. Their flat oar-like tails are used to propel them along through the open sea.

37

Sea iguanas lie in
the sun on the
rocks of the
Galapagos Island
in the South
Atlantic Ocean.

39

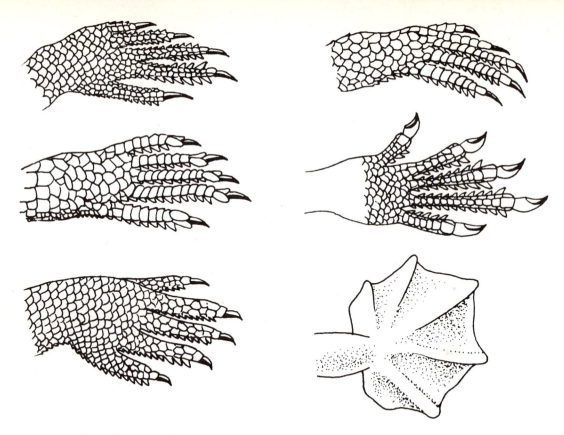

The feet of lizards which live in the desert. The gecko's foot (bottom right) *is like a snowshoe, and on the other feet the scales help the lizards stay on the surface.*

But the most adventurous methods of movement take place in the tree tops. The most famous performer is *draco*, the Indonesian flying lizard. Draco can glide short distances between trees by using a special flap of skin held out between the ribs. But no reptilian flying show would be complete without the oriental *golden tree snake*. This reckless animal has an outstanding double act which it performs at high level in the tree tops. After coiling itself up tightly this snake unwinds in such an explosive manner that with luck it will reach a branch on the next tree. If this appears dangerous, its next trick, for escaping its enemies,

Opposite: *A large African rock python drapes itself on a tree.*

The large and
monstrous monitor
lizard.

seems suicidal. Spreading out its ribs, drawing in its underside and holding its body rigid, the snake crash-dives to the ground below.

The sightings of monster snakes sixteen metres long are probably not real, though in the past the extinct snake *gigantophis* may well have been even longer than that. The world's longest snake today is the *reticulated python*, which is about ten metres long. The heaviest is the South American *anaconda*, which may tip the scales at over 135 kilos, twice the weight of an ordinary man. Jungle travellers are grateful that these huge snakes are not poisonous as well.

Another large snake is the *king cobra*, which is said to reach six metres in length. It is also a fast mover, and can inject more venom than any other snake. Because it has an unpleasant, aggressive manner, this snake is thought by some to be the world's most dangerous animal.

The accepted king of the lizards is the *komodo dragon*. Some of these have reached over three metres long and weigh about 160 kilos. There are claims from New Guinea that their local *monitor lizards* can be five metres long.

To some of us life might be less exciting if we had no hope of finding even larger reptiles. Colonel Fawcett claimed that in South America there were anacondas whose bodies were as thick as oil drums. Unfortunately he disappeared into the jungle, and has never been seen since.

43

Komodo dragons, the biggest lizards in the world.

Top: *The boa constrictor, which squeezes its prey to death;* centre: *the common viper;* below: *the deadly poisonous banded rattlesnake.*

46

5: Feeding Habits

All snakes feed on living creatures and are thus said to be *carnivorous*. In this they are rather handicapped by their unusual method of moving about. If you try crawling on the ground without using your hands and legs you will soon get tired. The snake also tires rapidly, and is unable to chase its prey for long distances. Instead it usually relies upon surprise, and the victim is disabled by a lightning attack.

Constricting serpents such as boas and kingsnakes entangle and squeeze their prey, which finally die by suffocation. Death by paralysis is the usual fate of the victims of the venomous snakes.

Poisonous snakes are skilled assassins. The most lethal are those with hinged front fangs, especially the North American pit vipers such as rattlesnakes. When a rattle-snake strikes it shoots its head forward, opening its jaws

and raising its fangs at the same time. On impact the hollow fangs penetrate the skin of the prey and the poison venom is injected. The snake speedily withdraws its head and may repeat the strike. The poison acts very fast and the prey, usually a rat or a mouse, dies quickly and does not seem to suffer much pain.

Snake venom is a special kind of saliva which contains a nerve or blood poison. The venom-injecting system is rather like a hypodermic syringe.

Unlike most other vertebrates, snakes have no legs or special teeth for tearing apart or chopping up the bodies of their victims. To make up for this the snake is capable of a remarkable feat. When it is stretched, the lower jawbone separates at the tip of the "chin" and makes a wide gap, which allows the prey to be swallowed whole.

For grasping and swallowing its meal the snake has special backward-curving teeth. Often the prey is so large that while swallowing it the snake finds it difficult to breathe. So to make sure that they have a good supply of air, snakes are able to push their windpipes forward, so that they act rather like snorkels.

As we saw earlier, snakes are handicapped by poor hearing. They are also rather short-sighted. These disadvantages might be very serious for an animal relying on surprise attack. But the snake makes up for them by having a highly developed sense of smell.

Snakes and lizards smell not only with their noses but

Opposite: *A puff adder stretches its mouth wide to swallow a rat.*

A grass snake swallows a frog. The snake's body can stretch hugely so that it can swallow its prey whole. Frogs and toads are the main food of grass snakes in England.

also with a unique organ in their mouths. When the snake flicks his tongue in its well-known way, it is picking up

scent particles from the air and ground. When the tongue

is returned to the mouth the snake tastes these particles with this special organ.

Although some snakes can use their excellent sense of smell to track down their victims, it is more usual for the camouflaged snakes to lie in wait for their unsuspecting prey, who sometimes almost blunder into them. The *Siamese swamp snake* is almost perfectly camouflaged. Covered in small plants and looking like a rotten log, this snake lurks with oriental cunning.

The *pit vipers* get their name from heat-sensitive hollows on the side of their heads. The pits are so sensitive to heat that they can pick out the slightest rise in temperature due to the approach of the smallest warm-blooded creature. This is a clever device for hunting by night.

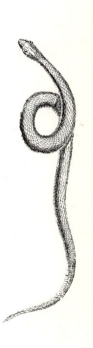

Below left, *an asp;* below right, *a banded krait, from India;* right, *a pit viper from Argentina. All these snakes are very poisonous, and lots of people die from their bites each year.*

The pit vipers are usually considered to be the most powerful of the North American snakes; but this honour should perhaps go to the *kingsnake*, which sometimes includes rattlesnakes in its diet.

Although many snakes feed on small mammals, lizards and even other kinds of snake, others have taken to more exotic foods. The small *thirst snakes* twist snails from their shells. Termites may have their insides sucked out by *thread snakes*, while the African snake *dasypeltis* swallows birds' eggs whole and spits out the broken shell fragments.

One of the strongest snakes is the Indian *rock python*. This snake has a large appetite and is known to swallow small deer and pigs. One even managed a leopard. Fortunately, humans are not normally eaten, but there are several rumours of young boys having been swallowed by pythons. One true story tells of a reticulated python that tried to devour a drunken man who had fallen asleep in a roadside ditch.

In comparison with snakes, the lizards are rather unexciting feeders. Nearly all of them eat insects.

The Australian *thorny devil* is a slovenly and ugly lizard. It spends much of its time sitting beside ants' pathways, lazily picking them off with its tongue as they go past. More energetic is the *crested dragon lizard*, which chases after flying insects. But the master of the insect eaters is the sharpshooting *chameleon*. Its tongue may be as long as itself, and has a sticky tip. In a flash

Desert battle between a snake and a kangaroo rat. The rat leaps about to stop the snake noticing where her young are hidden, and kicks sand into the snake's eyes. This battle was won by the rat, and the snake retreated.

this tongue can be shot out to trap an unsuspecting insect. The tasty morsel is then speedily carried to the mouth, which the animal snaps shut with a contented expression.

The most feared lizard is the *komodo dragon*. As its name suggests, this is a formidable animal. A recent expedition to their island home discovered that these huge lizards would even attack humans.

A few lizards are vegetarian. A good example is the marine iguana, which dives underwater to scrape seaweed off the rocks. Another lizard, the American *chuckwalla*, lives on a curious diet of flowers.

6: Barking Lizards and Immortal Snakes?

It is a well-known saying that attack is the best means of defence. A cornered venomous snake may strike and kill a menacing enemy with its poisonous fangs. Fortunately it is more common for snakes to try to escape and avoid the risk of damage to themselves.

Most snakes have many dangerous foes. In the folklore of rattlesnakes there are many stories of how these deadly snakes are the occasional victims of cats, dogs, wild turkeys, eagles and, surprisingly, mocking birds. A report from California described a golden eagle's nest which contained the remains of twenty-eight snakes. This number included a rattlesnake and a kingsnake.

Lizards are handicapped by being mostly harmless, and many try to bluff their way out of trouble. When the *toad-headed lizard* meets an enemy it immediately takes up a threatening stance. If this defensive bluff is called

Opposite: *How the chameleon gets its food. It shoots out its tongue, which is probably longer than itself, and catches insects which seem a safe way away.*

A fight to the death between a non-poisonous but immensely strong mussurana serpent *and a* jacarara, *one of the world's most venomous snakes. The serpent won at last, and ate its victim.*

the lizard tries to escape by burying itself as fast as it can.

The geckos are the only lizards which can make noises with their mouths. An amusing example is the *barking gecko*. It is only about six inches long but barks defiantly at humans. Of course this is like the small dog whose bark is much worse than his bite.

56 Instead of trying to bluff their enemies, many lizards

take flight and sprint to safety. In its escape the basilisk lizard almost performs miracles. After building up speed on land this animal can run several yards over water before it has to start swimming.

In contrast the *gila monster* needs no bluff or speed. It is one of the two types of poisonous lizard. It is, however, a slow-moving animal, and only uses its venom in self defence; so from the human point of view it is not a specially dangerous creature.

Some cobras have developed an especially dangerous

An Indian cobra. Notice the spectacle markings on its raised hood.

means of defence which has caught out even experienced snake catchers. These snakes can actually squirt a blinding venom through their fangs at their attackers' eyes. Another unusual defence is that found in the *spiny-tailed gecko*. This animal worries its enemies by squirting them with a sticky fluid from its tail.

When caught, some lizards can break off their tails. The lost tail then thrashes about and in the disturbance the lizard can sneak off while the enemy's attention is drawn to the tail.

Snakes and lizards often rely on camouflage for self-protection, but only a few lizards can actually change their skin colour. The chameleon has a skin which can alter its tone to match that of the surrounding vegetation. This animal is also flat shaped, and often sways from side to side, looking like a leaf in the breeze.

How some lizards escape. Their tails break clean off, and the owners can get away.

An African flap-necked chameleon *sheds its skin.*

This grass snake is trying to escape its attacker, a dog, by pretending to be dead and waiting till the dog loses interest and goes away.

Snakes and lizards differ from most other vertebrates in that their skin is a covering of scales. These scales are simply areas of thick skin joined together by thinner folds. It is these connections that makes the skin elastic and flexible.

Mammals, including humans, are always gradually replacing their skin as the surface wears away. The snakes and lizards, however, shed their old skins in one piece.

A defensive display by a frill-necked lizard, trying to frighten its enemy away.

The skin-shedding in snakes is so complete that even the clear layers of skin over the eyes are replaced.

Before shedding begins the skin becomes dull and the eyes mist over. The snake hides away at this time, and it may be partly because of its misty eyesight. Shedding of the skin often starts when the snake breaks the old dead layer of skin near the mouth. Then the snake slowly rubs its way forward and leaves behind the delicate cast skin.

61

When it emerges from its old skin the snake looks very bright and new. As we have seen, this led to the old belief that snakes never died. After each shedding the snake was thought to start life again.

This was firmly believed in earlier times, and many early writers wondered how the snake became immortal. One legend tells how God came and offered immortality to all the creatures of the earth. Unfortunately the visit was made at night when we and nearly all other animals were asleep. The watchful snake, which never closes its eyes, thankfully took advantage of the offer.

Other reptiles disguise themselves to trick their enemies. A, *a pipe snake* hides its head and waves its tail in the air*; B, a boomslang* inflates its throat*; C, an* armadillo lizard *with its tail in its mouth.*

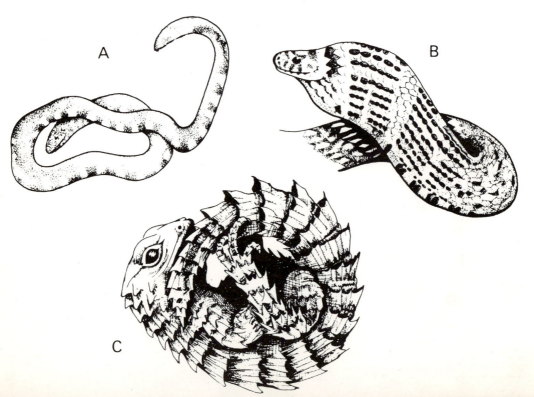

7: Snakes, Lizards and Men

In the past snakes were commonly used in European medicine. Extracts prepared from snakes' bodies were supposed to have all sorts of magical qualities. False remedies were available for anything from deafness to madness. At one time an uncanny snake tonic was even claimed to raise the dead. So highly was the snake valued that it became and remains the symbol of the medical profession.

In medicine snakes still have a use. Curiously enough, they are used to help cure snake bites. First the snake is carefully "milked" of its venom by squeezing its poison glands. Next, mammals are injected with a small amount of the venom. The dose is a very small one so that the animal does not suffer any severe ill-effects. Further doses are given and eventually the animal can take large quantities of the venom without ill effect. In this way the

"Milking" the fangs of a rattlesnake of its poison. Notice the forked tongue in the bottom of its mouth.

animal has built up an immunity to the effects of the poison. Finally small quantities of blood from these immune animals can be purified and used as a cure for human snake-bite victims. The only snag is that each cure may only work for one type of snake bite. So if you are unlucky enough to get bitten by a snake it is important to remember exactly what the snake looked like.

Everyone knows that after cutting yourself the blood usually clots and quickly seals off the injury. This is caused by a natural clotting chemical in the blood. The venom of some vipers contains something like this, so

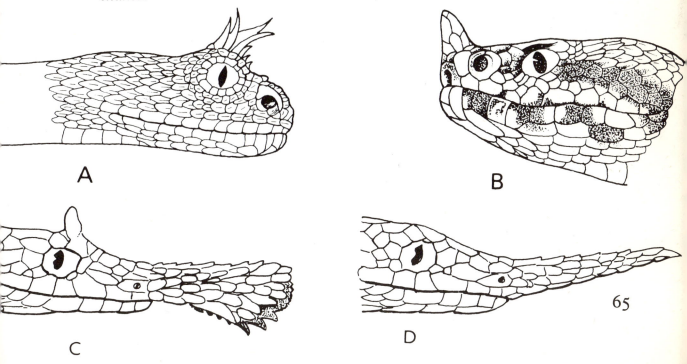

Strange snakes: A, *a horned adder from South-West Africa;* B, *a central European adder;* C *and* D, *female and male Madagascan snakes.*

65

a bite from one of these snakes can be dangerous. The chemical may cause our blood to clot inside the blood vessels, and death rapidly follows. On the other hand, the venom can be used to staunch bleeding in humans.

To most Europeans the idea of eating snakes is not very attractive. However, in Japan and parts of China snake flesh is considered to be a delicacy. Sea snakes especially are eaten in large quantities. In the Australian bush food may be in short supply and the Aborigines sometimes rely entirely on snake meat for their animal diet.

Nor do lizards escape the frying pan. In South America large iguanid lizards are cooked and eaten with great relish. The North American chuckwalla is the mealtime delight of the local Indians.

In a naval battle against the Romans, Hannibal thought up a devilishly cunning use for snakes. He hurled pots of poisonous serpents amongst the enemy oarsmen. This must have caused considerable panic below decks. Perhaps this was the origin of the phrase "to be put off one's stroke"! A more commonly known weapon is the poisoned arrow. The deadly tips are often coated with a mixture of snake venom and rotten liver.

On a more amusing note, visitors to Indonesia are warned to hold on to their headgear. From a vantage point in the trees the crafty local hat-thief skilfully dangles a gecko on a string. Because all geckos have very strong

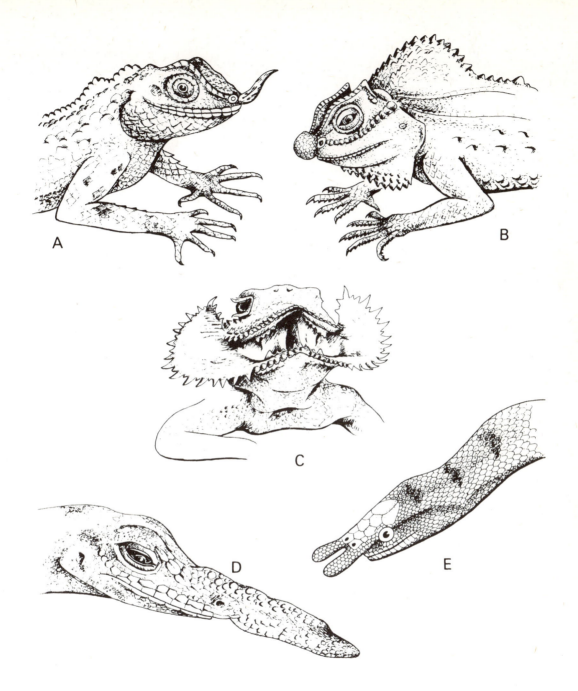

*More strange-looking snakes and lizards. A and B are lizards from
Ceylon; C, a sand lizard which is spreading the flaps at the side of
its mouth as a defence; D, a leaf-nosed anole lizard; and E, a
water snake with tentacles on its snout.*

A green lizard, common in garden hedges in Singapore, reaches out and clutches a flower.

gripping pads on their feet, the little animal may sometimes successfully grab a stranger's hat.

The worst enemy of all reptiles is probably man, and many handsome snakes and lizards are killed just for their skins. Most of these skins are used to make a variety of unnecessary fancy clothes and ornaments. Of course most people would prefer to see the animals alive, but

Opposite: *A large Eastern* coral snake *twined lazily round a tropical tree.*

despite this some snakes and lizards are being hunted to the verge of extinction. For instance, the Australian *lace monitor* lizard was becoming rather rare but is now fortunately protected in some states.

Another equally important problem is the loss of suitable places for the reptiles to live. The fast increasing numbers of people in the world need more food. This means that more and more wild areas are being turned over to farming. The development of more national parks would provide a safe place for the homeless natural inhabitants.

Good zoos also act as a safe home for many reptiles and many of them are now being bred in captivity. It may be that in the future these zoos will become important store houses for breeding animals that are becoming rare in their natural habitat.

The catching of zoo animals in the wild can be a hazardous job. One celebrated snake catcher was called Constantine Ionides. He survived and carried on despite thirteen dangerous snake bites and a kick on the head by an elephant. But he did become a little deaf.

It is said that the ancient Egyptians kept poisonous asps as house pets. It is unwise to follow this example as venomous snakes may bite accidentally, however carefully they are handled. Gilbert White, the great eighteenth-century naturalist, tells of a tame grass snake that was "as sweet as any animal while in a good humour."

70

Opposite: *The chameleon's* prehensile *tail works as a fifth leg, giving it something else to hold on with when it needs to.*

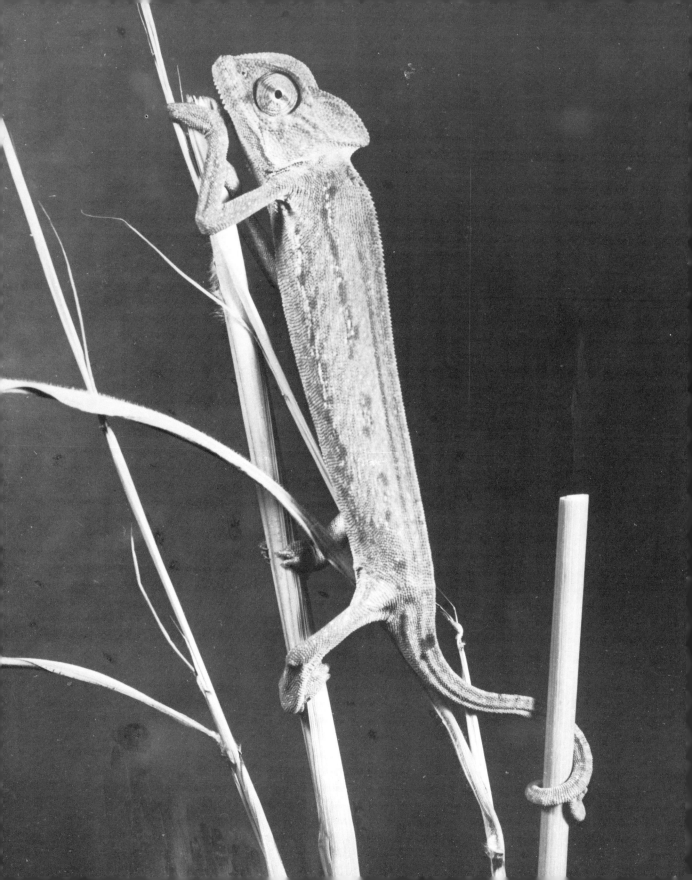

But as soon as it was alarmed, it "filled the room with such nauseous effluvia as rendered it hardly supportable." Here is a clear warning that grass snakes can raise domestic problems.

For the snake owner the most difficult problem is getting live food for their snakes' needs. The common grass snake, for instance, needs two live frogs a week; and few of us would wish to see a snake killing such engaging little creatures. The common European lizards make much pleasanter and easier pets because they can be fed

A freak of nature: this two-headed kingsnake in San Diego zoo in California lived for 6½ years. The snake had two lungs (usually they only have one) and two hearts as well.

on meal worms. Another possible reptile companion is the slow worm. These creatures are really legless lizards, and can be fed on small earthworms. One slow worm lived to the incredible age of 54 years in captivity.

Besides their feeding problems, snakes and lizards often die of disease in captivity. To avoid both these problems, the best thing is to keep them in captivity only for a few days and then release them where you found them. For this short stay put the animal in a large box or tank in a sunny place. Give it some pieces of wood or bark

An Egyptian *or* banded cobra *rears its handsome head.*

A sand goanna

for shade, and don't forget that the animals need a drink of water. Remember also that snakes and lizards are experts at escaping through narrow chinks.

An Emerald tree boa

Glossary

DINOSAUR. The name means *terrible lizard*. Many dinosaurs lived up to this description, for example the fearsome *tyrannosaurus* and the huge *brontosaurus*. But some dinosaurs were no bigger than chickens.

EMBRYO. The young of an animal in its developing stage before birth. The chick embryo gradually grows into the chick inside the bird's egg.

EVOLUTION. The process by which plants and animals gradually change and become better suited to their habitat. It is usually a very slow process, taking thousands and millions of years.

EXTINCTION. When a kind of animal dies out it becomes *extinct*, and can never be replaced; once it is gone it is gone for ever.

FANG. A special sharp hollow or grooved tooth for injecting venom.

FERTILIZATION. Before an egg will develop into an embryo it has to be *fertilized* by being joined with a male sperm.

FOSSILS. The remains or signs of an animal or plant that lived many years ago, now turned into, or marked on stone – for example bones, teeth, shells, footprints or droppings.

GECKOS. An attractive group of lizards, mostly nocturnal. They often live in human homes and are the only lizards that can utter sounds.

HIBERNATION. A very deep sleep that lasts all winter to avoid the cold and lack of food.

IMMORTALITY. Living for ever.

IMMUNE. Free or protected from an illness or poison. People who are injected with snake serum may become immune from the bite of that kind of snake.

MAMMALS. All animals that are warm-blooded and hairy. The young are born alive, not in eggs, and are fed on their mothers' milk.

NOCTURNAL. Coming out only at night.

REPTILE. The oldest and simplest of the true four-legged land animals. They lay eggs and live mostly in warm countries. Their skins are covered in scales and their blood temperature does not remain constant (like mammals) but rises and falls with the heat outside.

SERUM. A liquid made from the poison of a snake and used for injecting people against snake bites.

SPECTACLE. The transparent protective skin over the eyes of snakes.

VENOM. A special kind of saliva which often contains a blood or nerve poison. The snake injects it into the body of its prey through its fangs.

Finding Out More

The British reptiles are all rather timid creatures. Therefore you have to approach them very slowly in order to observe them in their natural habitat. At the slightest movement the common lizard normally retreats to a special hiding place. However, if you keep still, the animal will usually appear again after a few minutes. This is, of course, a good general piece of advice for watching most animals. By sitting still and being patient you will often see more than by walking for miles. With the common lizard this is especially important, because each of these little creatures may spend its whole life in a few square metres of ground.

In Europe the only dangerous reptile is the adder, and it should be left strictly alone. It can usually be recognized at once by the diamond-shaped markings on its back.

Some enthusiasts will not be satisfied with the small and perhaps less exciting British reptiles For these people the zoos can provide further interest and many contain some of the more spectacular snakes and lizards. Of the reptile houses perhaps the one in the London Zoo at Regent's Park is the best to see.

Museums sometimes have collections of stuffed and bottled reptiles. Sometimes these are attractively presented, but more often the appearance of the unfortunate creatures is likely to discourage interest.

Useful books:

Reptiles by Angus d'A. Bellairs (Hutchinson).

Australian Lizards by R. Bustard (Collins).

The Reptiles by Archie Carr (Time Life)

Snakes of the World by Raymond L. Ditmars (Macmillan).

Rattlesnakes by Frank J. Dobie (Little).

The World of Amphibians and Reptiles by Robert Mertens (Harrap).

The Reptile World by Clifford H. Pope (Knopf).

The Fascination of Reptiles by Maurice Richardson (Hill & Wang).

Picture Credits

The publishers thank the following for permission to use copyright pictures: Bruce Coleman Ltd, frontispiece, pp. 17, 21 (bottom), 34, 44–5, 48, 59, 60, 61, 64, 68, 73; Mary Evans Picture Library, title page, pp. 14, 26, 42, 46, 51; Frank W. Lane, pp. 6, 9, 18, 28, 30 (bottom), 32 (bottom), 54, 58, 69, 72, 74; Paul Popper Ltd, pp. 8, 21 (top), 32 (top), 50, 53, 56, 57; Natural History Photographic Agency, pp. 10, 12, 23, 38–9, 41, 71; Barnaby's Picture Library, pp. 22, 75. Drawings on pp. 16, 24, 29, 30, 31, 36, 37, 40, 62, 65, 67 by Angus Bellairs.

Index